- **Halloween T-shirt** — Paint design (pg. 124) on shirt. Add words using dimensional squeeze-bottle fabric paint. Sew buttons to shirt.
- **Backpack** — Paint design (pg. 114) on backpack. Sew ribbon bow and buttons to backpack.
- **Fall Vest** — Paint design (pg. 129) on vest. Fuse paper-backed fusible web to wrong side of fabrics. Cut patches out of fabrics; fuse to vest. Sew buttons to vest. Add "stitches" around hem of vest using permanent pen.

## PAGE 9

- **Christmas Sweatshirt** — Paint design (pg. 159) on shirt. Trim transfer close to edges of design. Cover painted design with transfer. Splatter paint shirt. Sew ribbon bows and jingle bells to shirt.
- **Stocking** — Paint design (pg. 147) on canvas stocking. Follow Making A Stocking Cuff (pg. 170) to make cuff. Fuse paper-backed fusible web to wrong side of fabrics. Cut patches out of fabrics; fuse to stocking and cuff. Hot glue buttons to stocking.
- **Patriotic Dress** — Paint design (pg. 122) on dress.
- **Card Holder** — Paint design (pg. 152) on canvas card holder. Add words using permanent pen. Insert dowel. Tie ribbon to dowel for hanger. Hot glue ribbon bow, artificial holly, and artificial snowflake to card holder.

## BACK COVER

- **Jewelry Box** — Paint design (pg. 94) on fabric. Fuse paper-backed fusible web to wrong side of painted fabric. Cut mat board to fit jewelry box insert. Using a pressing cloth, fuse painted fabric to mat board. Trim fabric to same size as mat board. Hot glue mat board to jewelry box. Secure jewel stones to fabric using puddles of dimensional squeeze-bottle glitter fabric paint. Hot glue ribbon bow to jewelry box.
- **Denim Jumper** — Paint designs (pg. 30) on jumper. Fuse paper-backed fusible web to wrong side of fabrics. Cut hearts out of fabrics; fuse to jumper. Follow Machine Appliqué (pg. 170) to secure appliqués to jumper. Secure lace and ribbon around bodice using clear nylon thread. Sew buttons to jumper.
- **Ladybug Wreath** — Paint design (pg. 82) on bristol board; cut out. Hot glue artificial flowers and leaves, ribbon bow, and design to grapevine wreath.
- **Photo Album** — Paint design (pg. 35) on fabric. Follow Steps 1-5 of Covering A Photo Album (pg. 170). Hot glue lace and ribbon lengths to front cover of album. Follow Steps 6-8 of Covering A Photo Album (pg. 170). Hot glue ribbon bows and button to album.

# GENERAL INSTRUCTIONS

## TRANSFERRING DESIGNS

Before transferring your design, use a small test transfer included in the book on a scrap of fabric or paper similar to your project to help you determine the best iron temperature and length of time needed to achieve a good transfer.

1. If you are transferring a design to a fabric item that will be washed, first wash and dry the item without using fabric softener; press.
2. Preheat the iron for five minutes on appropriate setting for item being used. Do **not** use steam.
3. Because the transfer ink may bleed through fabric, protect ironing board cover by placing a clean piece of fabric or paper on cover.
4. (**Note:** The inked transfer is the reverse of what will appear.) Place transfer, **inked side down**, on **right side** of fabric or paper. Place iron on the transfer; hold for five seconds. Do **not** slide iron. Pick up iron and move to another position on transfer so areas under steam holes are transferred. Carefully lift one corner of transfer to see if design has been transferred to item. If not, place iron on transfer a few more seconds.

### ALTERNATE METHOD FOR TRANSFERRING TO DARK ITEM:

Trace design onto tracing paper. Place tracing paper, **traced side down**, on right side of item; tape or pin in place. Insert a light-colored transfer paper (such as Saral®), **coated side down**, under tracing paper. Use a stylus or a dull pencil to draw over lines of design.

## PAINTING DESIGNS
### CHOOSING AND MATCHING PAINTS

If the item you are painting will be laundered, use either fabric paints or a mixture of half textile medium and half acrylic paint. If the item will not be laundered, use acrylic paint.

See the Cherished Teddies™ Color Palette (pg. 3) for color matching when choosing your paints. Hold the bottle next to the color you are trying to match. Most paints will dry a shade darker than they appear in the bottle. If you can't find an exact color match, find the closest color you can and add a small amount of white paint to make it lighter or a small amount of black paint to make it darker. Test color on a piece of fabric, canvas, or paper the same color as your project; let dry. If it is not right, keep adding small amounts of either white or black paint and testing until you get the right color.

### PAINTING PROJECTS

1. Stabilize fabric by ironing freezer paper (coated side toward fabric) to wrong side under design area. Place a waxed T-shirt form or a piece of plastic-wrapped cardboard beneath fabric; secure fabric with T-pins.
2. Test a fine-point permanent pen on a hidden area of your item to make sure ink does not bleed. Draw over all outlines and detail lines with pen. If you cover some detail lines when painting, lines can be redrawn after paint is completely dry.

**Continued on pg. 170.**

2

# Cherished Teddies™ Color Palette

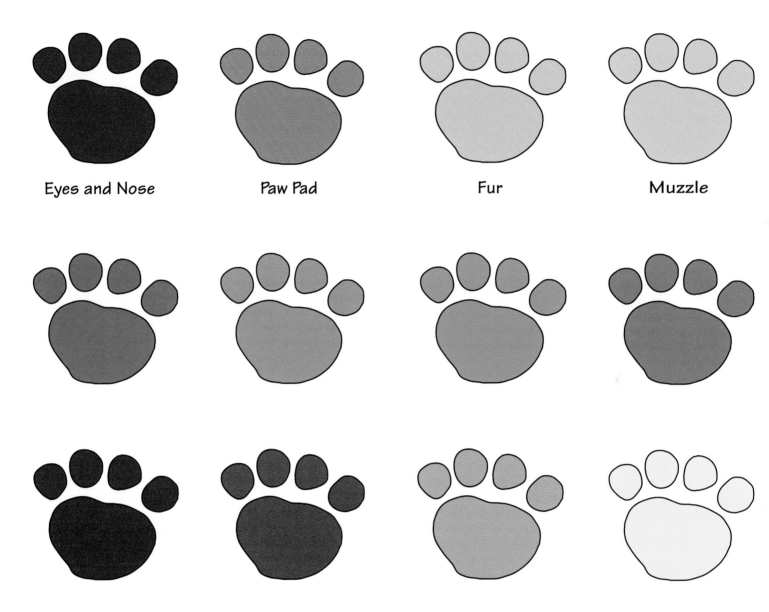

Eyes and Nose      Paw Pad      Fur      Muzzle

In order to re-create the charming look of Cherished Teddies™ characters, we've given you a color palette to help you choose your paint colors. The bear colors are labeled, but any of the colors shown may be used for clothing, accessories, and backgrounds.

There's No One Like Hue

My Country Tis Of Thee

CARDS

Test Transfer

Special Friends

Heidi and David

Special Friends

Friendship Blossoms

With Love

Friendship Blossoms
With Love

Daisy

A Little Friendship
Friendship Blossoms
With Love

A Little Friendship
Is A Big Blessing

*Phoebe*

The Book Of Teddies
A Little Friendship
Is A Big Blessing

# The Book Of Teddies

*Teddy and Roosevelt*

The Book Of Teddies

Our Friendship Will
Never Tumble

Jack and Jill

14

'O, You Go, Wherever You
I'll Follow

Tom, Tom The Piper's Son

Looking For A Friend
Like You

Little Bo Peep

I'm Plum Happy You're
My Friend

Little Jack Horner

I'm Plum Happy You're
My Friend

I'm Never Afraid With
You At My Side

Test Transfer

I'm Never Afraid With
You At My Side

Little Miss Muffet

You're Such A Good Friend
I'm Never Afraid With
You At My Side

You're A Honey Of A Friend

Kara

You're A Honey Of A Friend

Emily E. Claire

Kurtis D. Claw

"Sweethearts Forever"

Sweethearts Forever

*Craig and Cheri*

21

Sweethearts Forever

R. Harrison Hartford

Hillary Hugabear

# Railway Conductor

Lloyd

Railway Conductor

Mayor Wilson T. Beary

Bubblin' Over With Love

Betty

28

Love Surrounds Our
Friendship

Priscilla

Love Surrounds Our
Friendship

Test Transfer

Hearts Quilted With Love

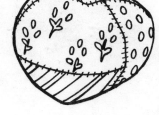

Amy

Side By Side With Friends

Test Transfer

Tracie and Nicole

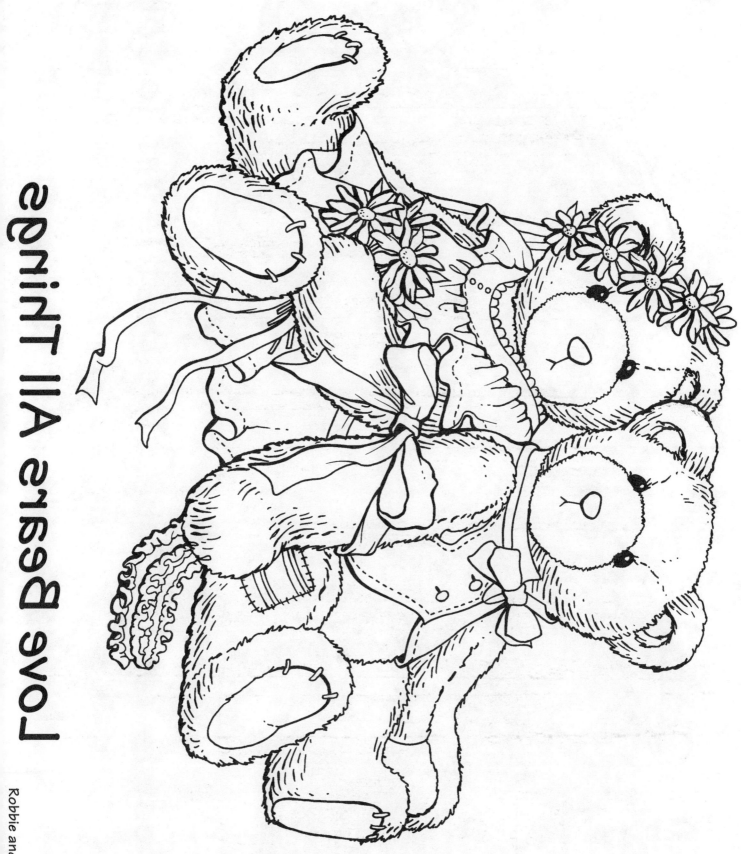

Love Bears All Things

Robbie and Rachel

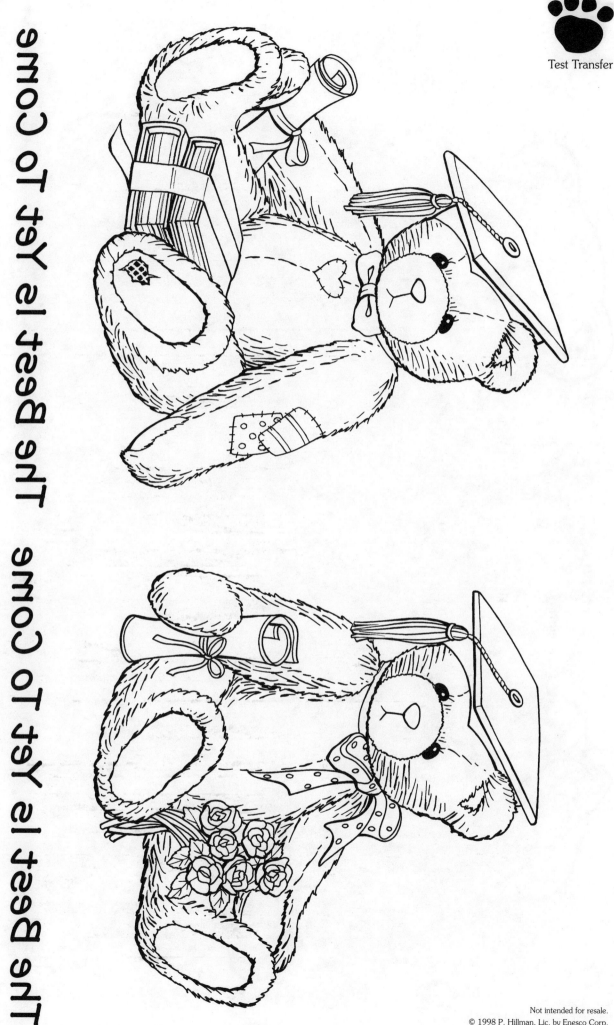

The Best Is Yet To Come

The Best Is Yet To Come

The Best Is Yet To Come  The Best Is Yet To Come

Our Friendship Is From  This Is Far From

Sea To Shining Sea  A Celebration

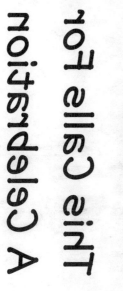

This Calls For
A Celebration

Our Friendship Is From
Sea To Shining Sea

Bob

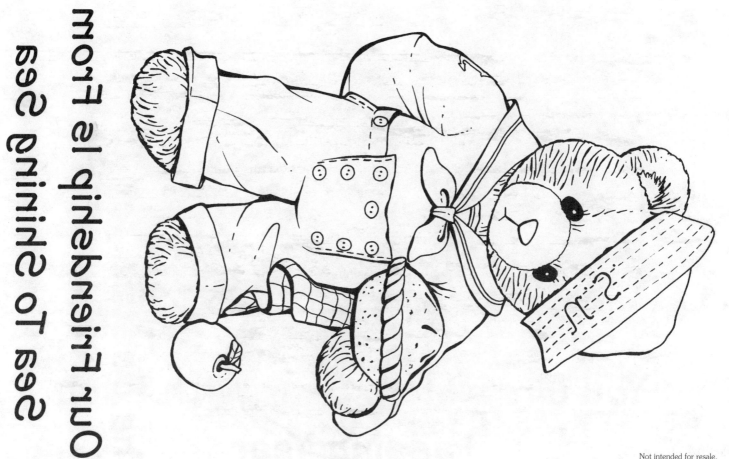

Test Transfer

Can't Bear To See You Under The Weather

Our Anniversary

You Grow More Dear With Each Passing Year

Christian

My Prayer Is For You

Christine

My Prayer Is For You

Test Transfer

Thank You For A Friend
That's True

Patrick

Thank You For A Friend
That's True

Test Transfer

Thank You For The
Sky So Blue

*Patrice*

Thank You For The
Sky So Blue

Test Transfer

Cradled With Love

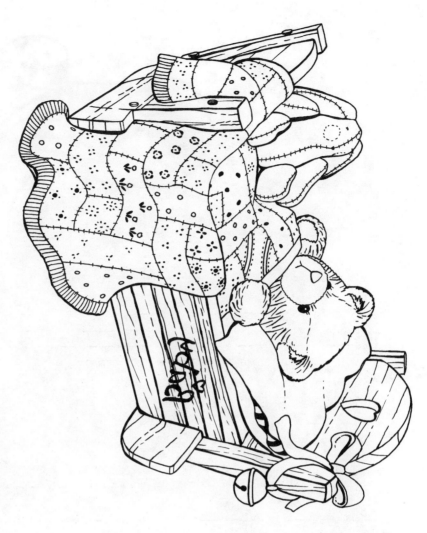

Holding On To
Someone Special

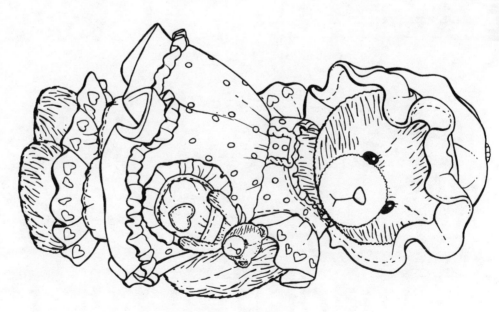

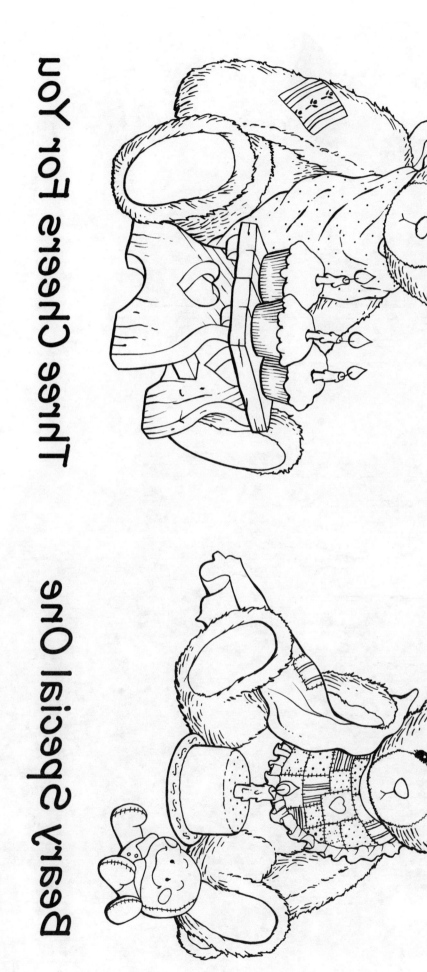

Three Cheers For You

Beary Special One

Little Fair Feather Friend

*Winona*

Untolding Happy Wishes
Four You

Child Of Kindness

A Little Friendship
To Share

Father

Mother

A Father Is The
Bearer Of Strength

A Mother's Love
Bears All Things

44

Young Son

Older Son

Child Of Hope

Older Daughter

Child Of Pride

Child Of Love

Thomas

Jonathan

Harrison

Chuggin' Along

Sail With Me

We're Going Places

Our Friendship Is A Perfect Blend

Freda and Tina

Special Friends

My Beary Best Friend

Elizabeth and Ashley

My Beary Best Friend
The Best Friends

Special
Friends

Old Friends Are
The Best Friends

Christopher

48

Test Transfer

Yesterday's Memories Are
Today's Treasures

*Zachary*

Yesterday's Memories Are
Friends That Live A Far Apart
Today's Treasures

Friends Are Never Far Apart

Beth and Blossom

Friends Are Never Far Apart

Heart To Heart

It's Twice As Nice With You

Nathaniel and Nellie

52

It's Twice As Nice With You

Bear Hugs

Beth

Bear Hugs

There's No One Like Hue

There's No One Like Hue

54

Priscilla Ann

Test Transfer

There's No One Like Hue

Life Is Sweet, Enjoy

Benji

Annie, Brittany, Colby, Danny and Ernie
Page 2 of 2

57

# Riding Across The Great White North

Preston

I Picked The Beary Best
For You

*Diane*

Test Transfer

Everything's Coming
Up Roses

Rose

Love Stems From
Our Friendship

Susan

Not intended for resale.
© 1998 P. Hillman, Lic. by Enesco Corp.

60

Spring Brings A Season
Of Beauty

Love Stems From
Our Friendship

Everything's Coming
Up Roses

Megan

Test Transfer

Spring Brings A Season
Of Beauty

Megan

Spring Brings A Season
Of Beauty!

Summer Brings A Season Of Warmth

Kimberly

62

Summer Brings A Season
Of Warmth

Test Transfer

Autumn Brings A Season
Of Thanksgiving

Hannah

Winter Brings
A Season Of Joy

Gretchen

Winter Brings
A Season Of Joy

My Heart Wishes For You

Darla

Won't You Be My Sweetheart

Jilly

Friendship Keeps Me
On My Toes

Mindy

Love Unveils A
Happy Heart

Darrel

Friendship Keeps Me
On My Toes

Love Unveils A
Happy Heart

Cozy Tea For Two

Thelma

Cozy Tea For Two

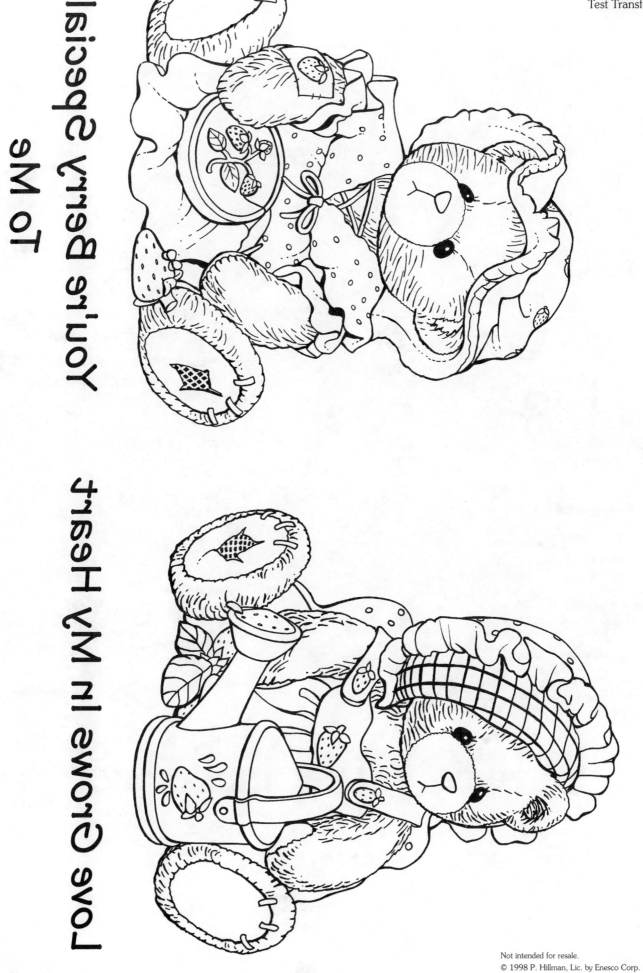

You're Berry Special
To Me

Jenna

Love Grows In My Heart

Ella

70

You're Berry Special
To Me

Love Grows In My Heart

In Grandmother's Attic

Tasha

Jacki

Sara

Karen

Hugs And Kisses

Love Ya

Best Buddy

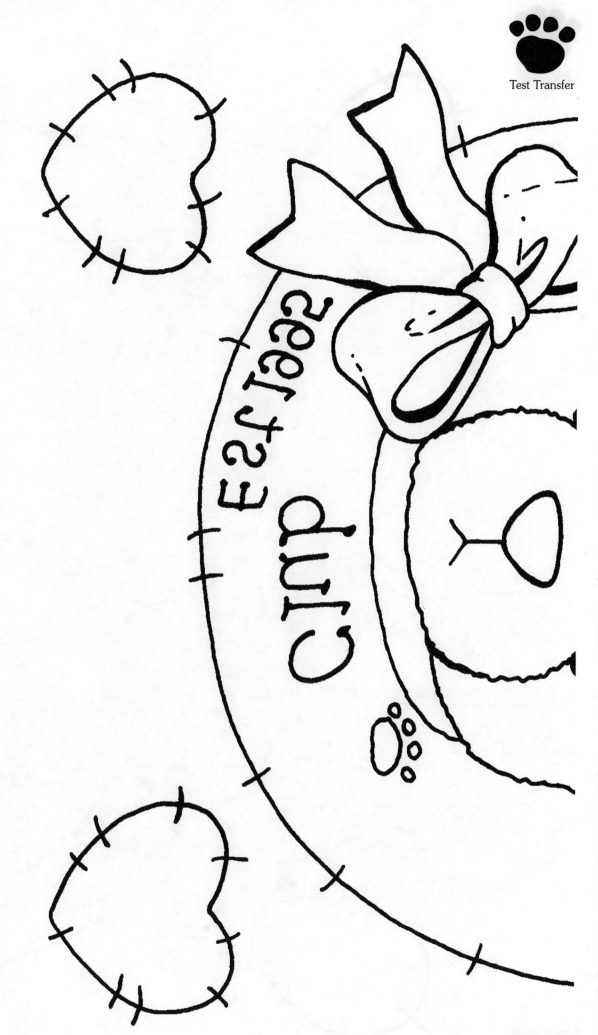

East Seas Club

73

Cherished Teddies

74

"Bee" My Friend

*Bea*

"Bee" My Friend

Kiss The Hurt And
Make It Well

You're Tops With Me

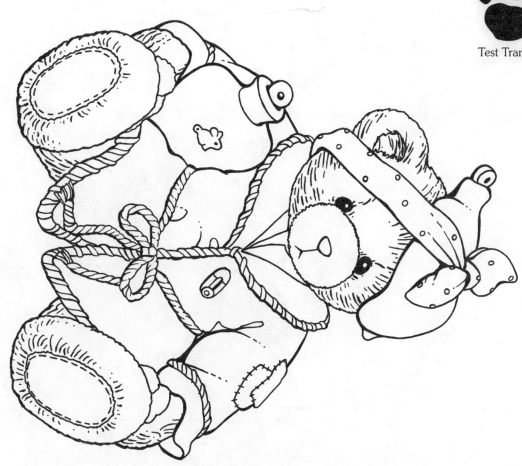

Kiss The Hurt And
Make It Well

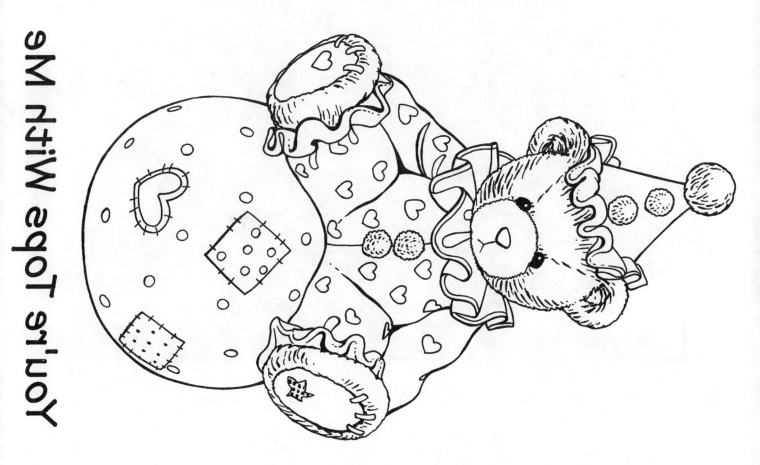

You're Tops With Me

Wally

Test Transfer

Love Is A Bear Necessity

Logan

# Trunk Full Of Bear Hugs

Seal Of Friendship

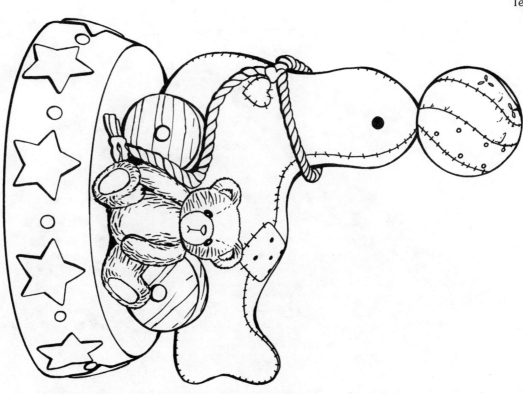

You Take Center
Ring With Me

Step Right Up
And Smile

Claudia

Bruno

Seal of Friendship

Step Right Up
And Smile

You Take Center
Ring With Me

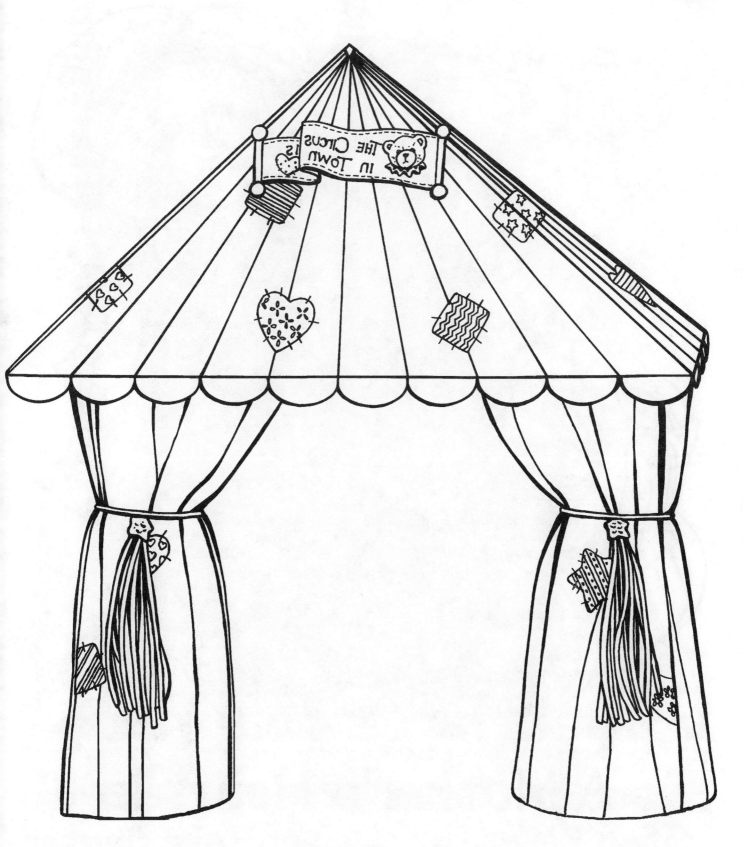

**80**

A Mother's Heart Is
Full Of Love

Jessica

Bless A Mother's Heart Is Near
Full Of Love

Blessings Bloom When You Are Near

Violet

82

Test Transfer

You Make Wishes Come True

Kittie

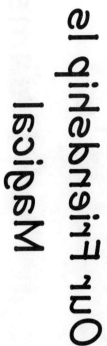

Our Friendship Is
Magical

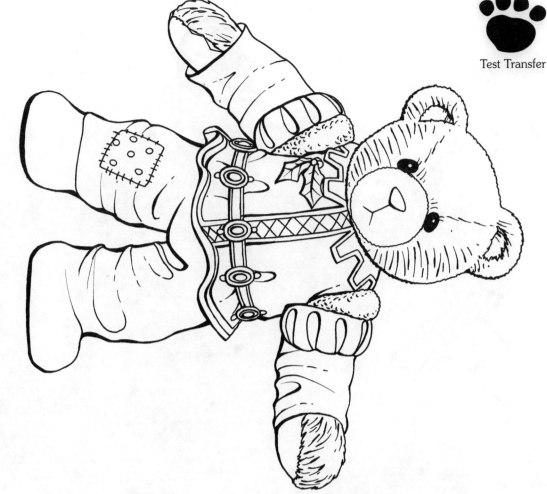

Making Holiday Wishes
Come True

Our Friendship Is
Sugar Magic Beams

Making Holiday Wishes
Come True
Beary Santa

Sugar Plum Dreams

Clara

I'll Keep You Beary Safe

Mouse King

Two Friends Mean Twice
The Love

Allison and Alexandria

We're Beary Good Pals

Seth and Sarabeth

We're Beary Good Pals
Our Hearts Belong To You

Our Hearts Belong To You

*Priscilla and Greta*

A Cup Full Of Love

Margaret

My Best Is Always You

Lisa

Test Transfer

You Have Touched My Heart

91

*Jasmine*

Friendship Is A Cozy Feeling

Test Transfer

92

Michael and Michelle

Hooray For You

*Anna*

93

Hooray For You

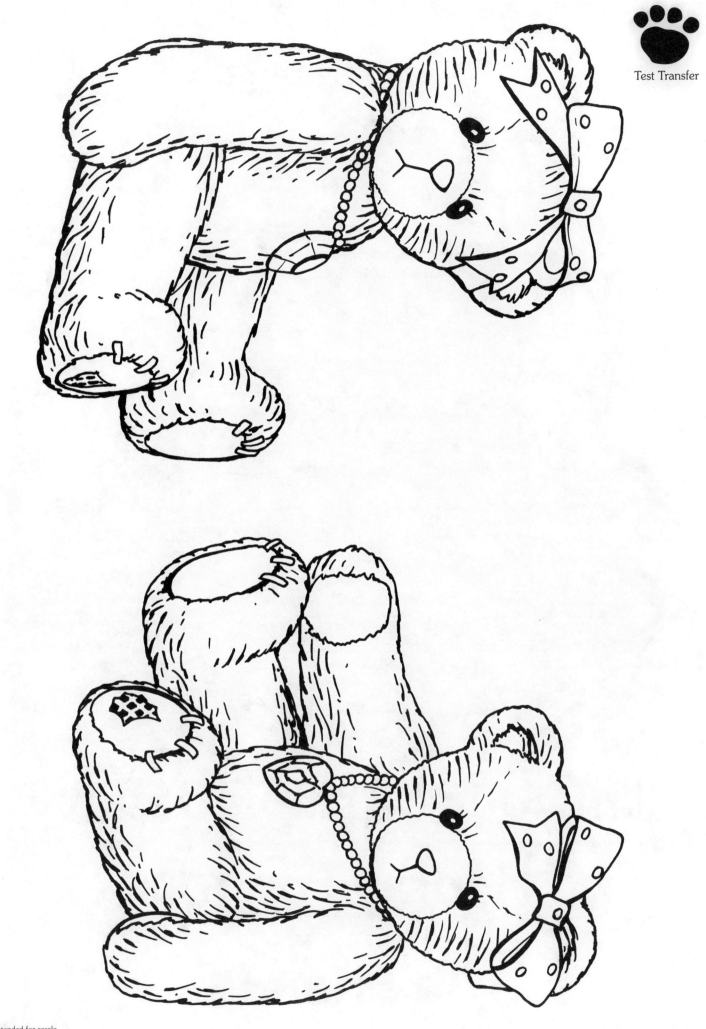

I'm Your Bathing Beauty

Judy

I'm Your Bathing Beauty
Everything Pale in
Comparison
To Friends

Everything Pails In
Comparison
To Friends

*Gregg*

Everything Pales My
San&Comparison You
To Friends

Test Transfer

There's Room In My
Sand Castle For You

Sandy

There's Room In My
Sand Castle For You

Test Transfer

# Underneath It All
## We're Forever Friends

*Jim and Joey*

Ready To Make A Splash

Jerry

Ready To Make A Splash

You're My Shooting Star

Larry

Let's Hear It For Friendship!

Debbie

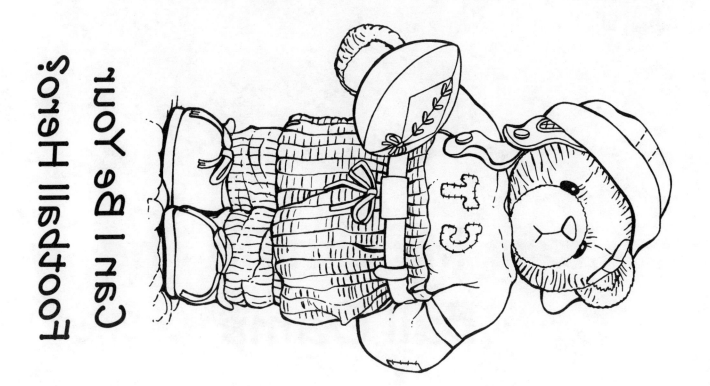

Football Hero?
Can I Be Your

Butch

# Take Me Out To The
# Ball Game

Lou

We Take Me Out To The
Ball Game

Test Transfer

We Make A Winning Team

Not intended for resale.
© 1998 P. Hillman, Lic. by Enesco Corp.

Whitney

103

We Make A Winning Team

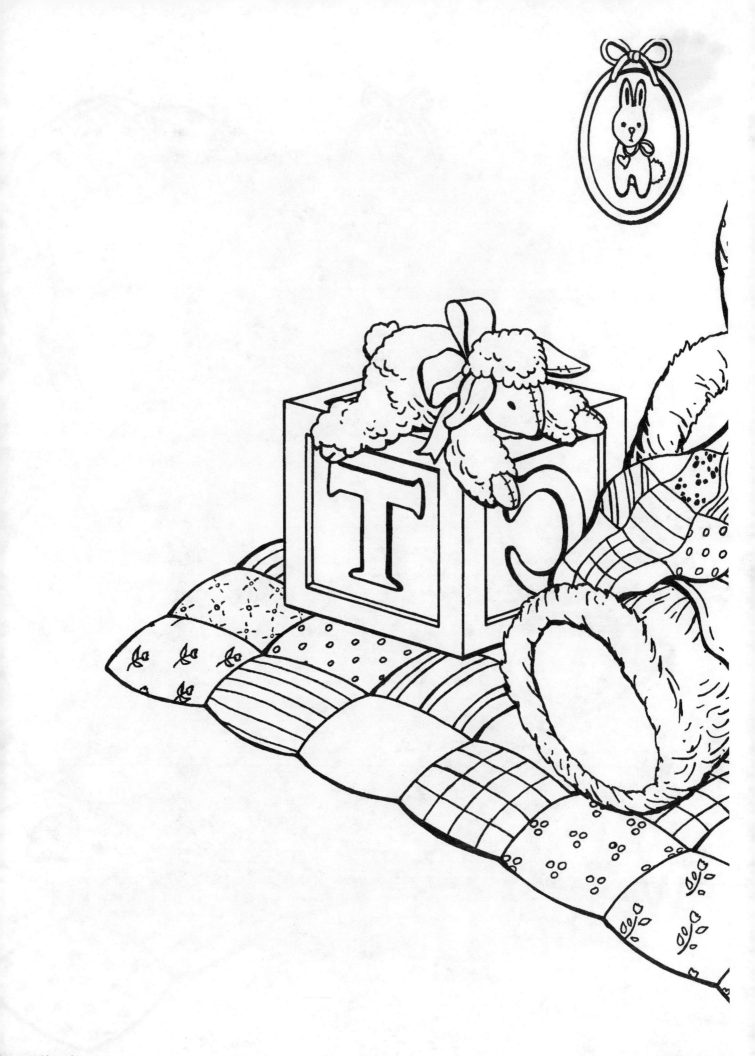

A New Year With
Old Friends

*Jack*

A New Year With
Old Friends

Be Mine

*Phoebe*

107

Friendship Is In The Air

Mark

Friendship Is In The Air
Showers Of Friendship

Showers Of Friendship

Alan

Showers Of Friendship

Friendship Is In Bloom

May

Friendship Is In Bloom

Planting The Seed Of
Friendship

June

Planting The Seed Of
Friendship

A Day In The Park

Julie

Smooth Sailing

Arthur

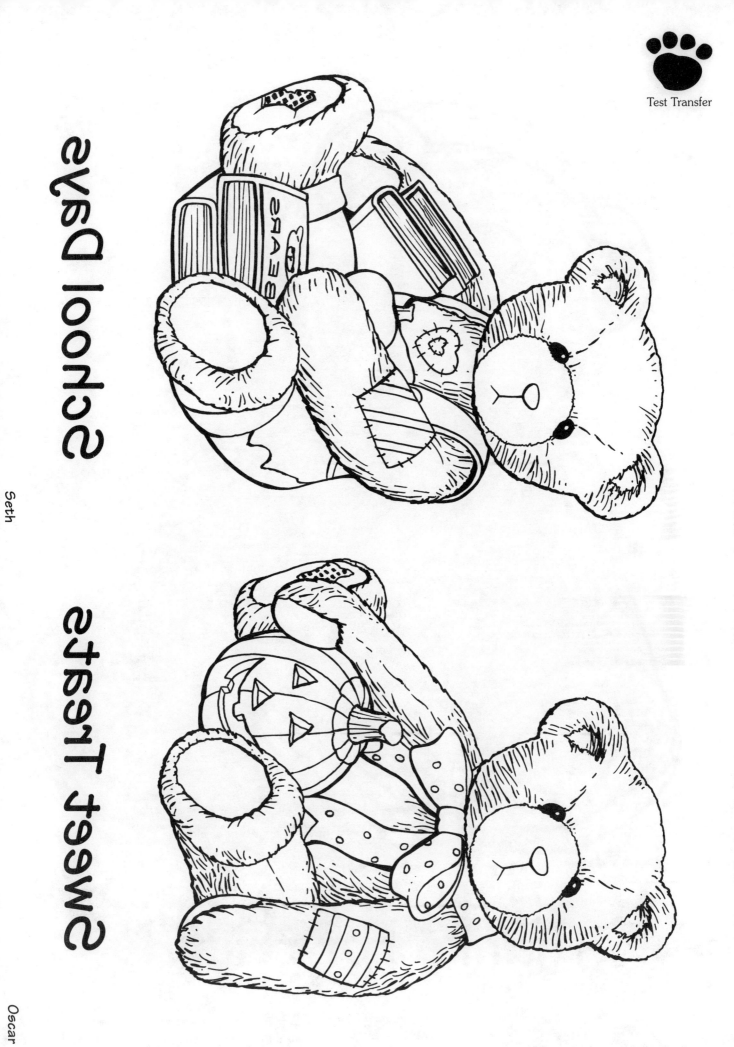

School Days

*Seth*

Sweet Treats

*Oscar*

Thanks For Friends

*Nicole*

Happy Holidays, Friend
Thanks For Friends

Happy Holidays, Friend

*Denise*

Luck Found Me A Friend

Happy Holidays, Friend

Luck Found Me A Friend
In You

*Sean*

Test Transfer

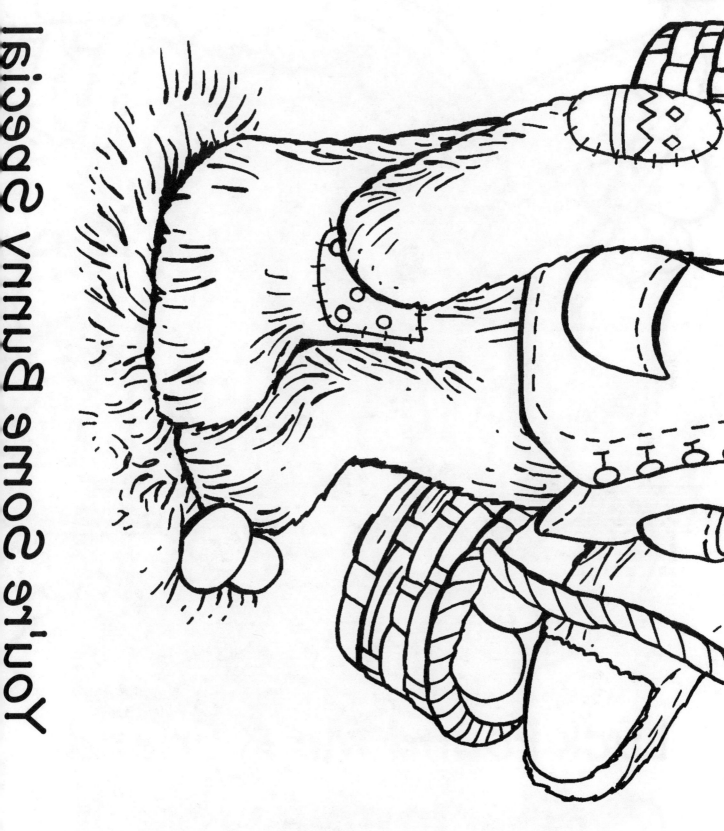

Springtime Happiness

Our Love Is Ever-blooming

Our Love Is Ever-blooming

My Country Tis Of Thee

Libby

My Country Tis Of Thee

I Want You...

To Be My Friend

I Want You...
To Be My Friend

Sam

I Want You...
You Light My Spirit
To Be My Friend

You Lift My Spirit

Stacie

You Have A Special Place
In My Heart

Andy

125

You Have A Special Place
In My Heart
Be Extinct

Test Transfer

Our Friendship Will Never
Be Extinct

Rex

Ya I'm Batty Over You...

Our Friendship Will Never

Be Extinct

I'm Batty Over You

Barry

127

I'm Batty Over You

You're My Little Pumpkin

Test Transfer

Daniel

You're My Little Pumpkin

Falling For You

Pat

Falling For You

An Autumn Breeze Blows
Blessings To Please

Cathy

An Autumn Breeze Blows
Blessings To Please

How I Love Being Friends
With You

*Brenda and Buckey*

How I Love Being Friends

With You

Glory To The Newborn King

Test Transfer

Glory To The Newborn King

*Grace*

Glory To The Newborn King

I Brought The Star

Angie

I Brought The Star

A Season Filled With Sweetness

To The New Millennia

A Season Filled With Sweetness

Steven

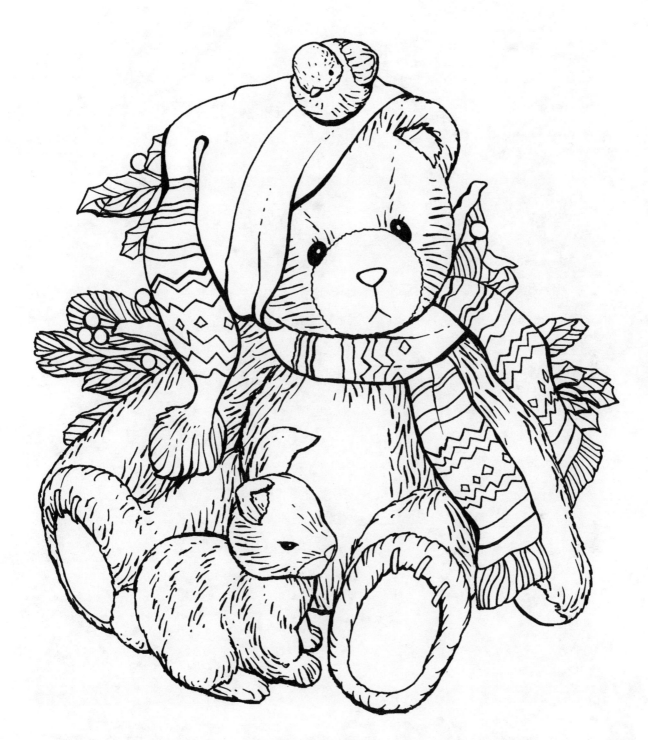

# The Spirit Of Friendship Warms The Heart

*Charlie*

Bearer Of Good Tidings

Klaus

Bearer Of Good Tidings

Catchin' The Holiday Spirit!

Holden

Hark The Herald
Angels Sing

An Angel to Watch
Over You

Friends Are Always Pulling For You

Erica

Homemade Love

A Cup Of

Holly

I'm All Wrapped Up In Your Love

Jamie and Ashley

Walking In A Winter
Wonderland

Lindsey and Lyndon

Walking In A Winter
Wonderland
It's A Holiday On Ice

It's A Holiday On Ice

Adam

143

I'll Play My Drum For You

Ronnie

I'll Play My Drum For You

**145**

Test Transfer

All Paths Lead To Kindness
And Friendship

Sven and Liv

All Paths Lead To Kindness
Up On the Rooftop
(And Friendship)

Up On The Rooftop

Kris

Up On The Rooftop

I'm Head Over Skis For You

I'm Head Over Skis For You

I've Fallen For You!

ot intended for resale.
1998 P. Hillman, Lic. by Enesco Corp.

*Spencer*

Test Transfer

Cup Full Of Love

Joann

Cup Full Of Peace

Jean

Cup Full Of Joy

*Jordan*

**151**

Friendship Never
Melts Away

Mitch

Test Transfer

Going My Way For
The Holidays

James

© 1998 P. Hillman, Lic. by Enesco Corp.

Skating On Holiday Joy

*Candace*

Skating On Holiday Joy

Bear Tidings Of Joy

Bear Tidings Of Joy

Eric

Snow Fun When You're

Bear Nodding Angel of Joy

Test Transfer

Snow Fun When You're
Not Around

Ted

Snow Fun When You're
Not Around

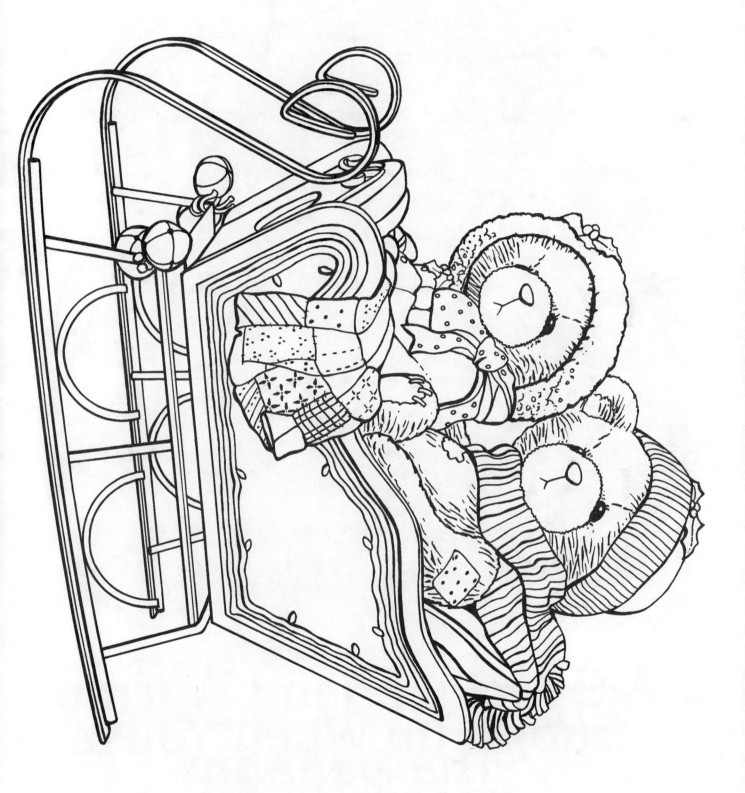

A Special Friend Warms
The Season

Mary

Test Transfer

Cozy Warm Wishes
Coming Your Way

*Alice*

Warm Hearted Friends
Cozy Warm Wishes
Coming Your Way

Warm Hearted Friends

intended for resale.
998 P. Hillman, Lic. by Enesco Corp.

Earl

Warm Hearted Friends

Friends In Toyland

Friends In Toyland

Hans

Friends In Toyland

All Aboard The
Santa Express

Lionel

Test Transfer

You're A Bear's Best Friend

Ted

You're A Bear's Best Friend

Striking Up Another Year

intended for resale.
998 P. Hillman, Lic. by Enesco Corp.

Jeffrey

Striking Up Another Year
With Cheer

Ringing In The New Year
With Cheer

Newton

Happy New Year

Ringing In The New Year
With Cheer

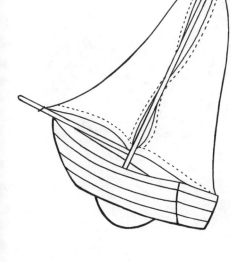

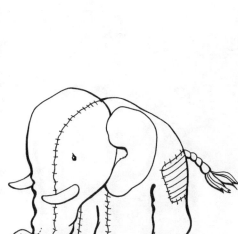

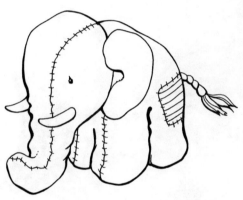

Test Transfer

ABCDEFGHI
JKLMNOPQ
RSTUVWXYZ

abcdefghi
jklmnopq
rstuvwxyz

ABCDEFGHI
JKLMNOPQ
RSTUVWXYZ

abcdefghi
jklmnopq
rstuvwxyz

A B C D E F G H I
J K L M N O P Q
R S T U V W X Y Z

a b c d e f g h i
j k l m n o p q
r s t u v w x y z

A B C D E F G H I
J K L M N O P Q
R S T U V W X Y Z

a b c d e f g h i
j k l m n o p q
r s t u v w x y z